Pretty Serious Job-Hunting Stuff

Written and illustrated by
Robert Fairview

Copyright © 2022 Robert Fairview. All Rights Reserved.

***

The author's personal stories presented in this book are true. The names have been changed to protect the identities of the people involved.

***

DISCLAIMERS

This publication is intended to inform and entertain only. The author makes no guarantee that a reader will find a job by following the suggestions provided. The author shall not be held liable for any loss incurred from the usage of this publication.

Searching for a job is a stressful experience that may cause headache, nausea, vomiting, diarrhea, insomnia, heart palpitations, or depression. Seek medical attention if you experience any of these symptoms while reading this book. Please consult a physician before embarking on a strenuous job-hunting program.

***

ISBN 9798423768980
Independently Published

Contact: fairviewr@yahoo.com

Contents

Introduction 1

1. Getting Started 3

    Why Are You Looking for a Job? 3

    The Elusive Good Job 5

    Identifying Good Jobs for You 7

    Job Evaluation Table 10

    What Do You *Not* Want To Do? 18

2. Understanding Business 23

    Capitalism 24

    Busy-ness 25

    Banking 26

    Marketing 28

    Gross Domestic Product (GDP) 32

    Trickle Down Economics 33

    Corporations and the Stock Market 34

    Supply and Demand 38

3. The Search Is On 41

    The Job Market 41

    The Waiting Game 45

    Networking 47

Resumes 49

Cover Letters 57

The Launch 57

Interpreting Job Ads 60

4. Interviews 65

The Ultimate Sales Job 65

Interview Scenarios 68

Why Are They Hiring? 71

Interview Steps 74

A Winning Strategy 76

Interview Questions 80

Strange Interviews 83

Other Ramblings 85

5. You Found a New Job 91

Quitting Your Present Job 91

Your Last Days 95

The First Day in Your New Job 97

The First Weeks in Your New Job 100

The Cycle Repeats 103

Introduction

As someone who has worked in the business world for decades, I have gone through the job-hunting and hiring process many times, not only as a job hunter but also as an advisor to management trying to select new employees. The process can be exceptionally grueling for job seekers because most jobs today are very specialized, and companies are extremely selective.

Adding to the difficulty is the fact that Human Resources people and managers, who ultimately make the hiring decisions, are increasingly clued out about the work details and skills required to do the jobs they are trying to fill. The main challenge in finding work today is convincing these people that you are useful to them.

In the following chapters, I will help you tackle the job-hunting challenge by taking you on a journey through the entire hiring process. By understanding the process, you will have a better chance of landing a suitable job. In the chapter on business fundamentals, I explain that we are all small components (workers) in a large machine (the economy), and you must know how the machine works before you can troubleshoot problems.

Unlike many job-hunting books, this book is short and does not ask you to complete a lot of difficult assignments. However, you can still learn some pretty serious job-hunting stuff (and possibly get a few chuckles) by studying the following chapters. With that being said, let's get to work finding you a decent job.

1. Getting Started

Why Are You Looking for a Job?

I know you are eager to start searching for your dream job, but before we begin, you need to answer an important question: Why do you want a job in the first place? Do you realize that people who have jobs are a strain on the environment? They need cars, gas for their cars, clothes for work, etc. They eat in restaurants more often because they are too tired to cook dinner at home after working in their dreadful jobs all day. They are always shopping for more and more stuff. They overload the infrastructure by congesting the roads, filling the buses and subways, packing the restaurants, and crowding the stores.

If you are unemployed, you need far less. You don't need a car. The only clothes you need are a pair of sweatpants and a couple of T-shirts. Underwear is optional. You certainly don't travel. You have a much smaller carbon footprint. In addition, you have more time to exercise and stay in shape, more time to read and learn new hobbies, and more time to clean and fix things around your home (although you most likely won't do any of those activities even if you have the time).

Alas, though I am sure you would love to stay in bed all day, the reality of modern life requires that you find a job eventually. The standard reasons are:
- Your parents are pressuring you and threatening to kick you out of the house unless you get a job and quit being a mooch.
- Your spouse is pressuring you and threatening to kick you out of the house unless you get a job and quit being a mooch.
- Your other relatives or friends are pressuring you and threatening to kick you out of the house unless you get a job and quit being a mooch.
- Your landlord, utility companies, credit card companies, and car finance company are threatening to do something drastic unless you pay them some money.
- Your Unemployment Insurance benefits or COVID relief benefits are ending.

If you already have a job, you are probably unhappy and want to find a better job (your main reason for reading this book, I assume). I can relate, having spent many years myself working in dysfunctional companies surrounded by disgruntled co-workers. In fact, recent surveys show that more than half of workers today are dissatisfied in their jobs, so you are not alone.

I have analyzed this epidemic of employee dissatisfaction occurring in the workplace, and I attribute most worker discontent to one or more of the following factors:

- The inherently unpleasant tasks that must be performed.
- The frantic pace and excessive amount of work that is expected.
- The turmoil caused by the lunatic managers who are in charge.
- The frustration of working with co-workers who are lazy, incompetent, or just plain nasty.
- The lack of flexibility and the disregard of employers for the personal lives of employees.
- The improper tools, equipment, and technology that must be used.
- The lack of stability and job security.
- The lack of career advancement.
- The lack of recognition and reward received for good work.
- The pathetic wages.
- All of the above.

If all of the above applies to your own situation, it's time for you to be looking for a better job. I hope that reading this book helps.

The Elusive Good Job

I frequently overhear people in general talking about someone having a good job. A middle-aged woman will mention, "My son has a good job with the government."

A single woman telling her friend about a recent date will excitedly say, "He's cute, and he has a really good job at the bank."

A young man having a conversation with his friend will remark, "My cousin got a good, high-paying job in construction."

What do people actually mean when they refer to a "good job"? Many people define a good job simply as a job that pays a lot of money. In today's overly materialistic society, having a high income seems to be the priority. If money is the only criterion, though, being a drug dealer is a good job because drug dealers often make enormous amounts of money. However, they also have a high probability of being raped in prison or being murdered on the street. It doesn't sound like a very good job to me.

Ask a politician in the majority party for a definition of a good job, and he or she will likely answer that any job created by the economic policies of the current government is a good job. Every month statisticians release reports on the number of jobs created (or lost) in the economy. Politicians never talk about the quality of the newly created jobs. As long as jobs are continually being created to pay taxes to fuel government spending, politicians are happy.

The definition of a good job has changed with time. One hundred years ago, a job working twelve hours per day that paid enough to avoid starvation was thought to be a good job. Of course, some people think that definition still applies today. A century ago, a job in a mine or a factory enduring horrid conditions and constant exposure to toxic materials was considered a good job. Again, some people believe that those are good jobs today.

Nevertheless, workers' expectations have gradually changed in the developed world because of advancements in technology and improvements in general living standards. Working people today don't consider subsistence living adequate. We are more educated and more affluent, and we expect more from our jobs. We want more than the mere crumbs left over from the wealthy; we want the scraps, too!

The definition of a good job also varies greatly depending on an individual's likes, dislikes, personality, and goals. One person's idea of a good job is someone else's idea of a terrible job. However, some jobs are almost universally seen as good, and some jobs are generally seen as bad. For example, nearly everyone agrees that celebrities in professional sports, movies, TV, and music have good jobs. These people are rich and famous, and they love their work. Unfortunately, these jobs represent only about .00001% of the job market. On the other end of the scale, we have telemarketing jobs, which are normally seen as bad jobs. Telemarketers are not only paid minimum wage but also hated by everyone else on the planet. Judging from the number of phone calls I receive, I estimate that telemarketing jobs make up over 50% of today's job market.

Identifying Good Jobs for You

The first step in your job search is to identify jobs that you deem good and jobs that are not so good. Your answers to the following questions will help in making that assessment.

Which of the following categories is most appealing to you?
a. Helping others (e.g., nurses, teachers, and social workers).
b. Creating things (e.g., artists, writers, and designers).
c. Building things (e.g., tradespeople, construction workers, and factory workers).
d. Working with information (e.g., computer programmers and accountants).
e. Being a pushy know-it-all, bossing people around, and telling everybody what to do (e.g., managers, project leaders, executive secretaries, and my dental hygienist).
f. Swindling people out of their money (e.g., car salespeople, residential contractors, real estate agents, and anyone who works in the financial services industry).

Which of the following activities do you prefer to do?
a. Work at a desk (sit in front of a computer all day; get fat and hunchbacked; get carpal tunnel syndrome).
b. Do physical work (be on your feet all day; lift heavy objects; get knee, shoulder, neck, and back problems).
c. Operate machinery (sit all day; get fat; breathe in diesel exhaust all day; die young).
d. Travel for business (sit in cars, planes, airports, meetings, restaurants, and bars; get divorced; drink yourself to death).
e. Wander around aimlessly and try to look busy (e.g., retail sales associates and all engineering managers I have ever known).

Which of these scenarios do you find most desirable?
a. Working in quiet isolation where nobody talks, and all you hear is the faint sound of keyboard strokes and mouse clicks (e.g., accounting, IT, and most engineering departments).

b. Listening all day to people complaining and whining (e.g., customer service).
c. Being exposed to the constant sound of machinery (e.g., factory work and construction work).
d. Listening to nonstop cursing and swearing (e.g., all male-dominated jobs).
e. Hearing bar glasses tingling (e.g., sales).

Which work environment do you favor?
a. Mindless drudgery (e.g., factory work, engineering, accounting, and government work).
b. Frantic pandemonium (e.g., customer service, purchasing, shipping/receiving, transportation, retail at specific times of the year, restaurants at specific times of the day, and hospitals at most times).
c. Golfing and drinking (e.g., sales).

Which of the following do you wish to be?
a. A problem solver—someone who tries to solve problems or spends most of his or her time fixing the mistakes made by others (e.g., customer services reps, service and repair people, and competent tradespeople).
b. A problem creator—someone who creates large problems by trying to solve small or imaginary problems (e.g., sales and marketing people, engineers, industrial designers, chemists, financial services people, managers, scientists, and politicians).
c. A problem recorder—someone who records problems but does nothing about them or has no power to do anything about them (e.g., quality control personnel, accountants, statisticians, government workers, and news/media people).

Job Evaluation Table

After you have answered the previous questions, you should be able to evaluate various jobs to determine if they are "good jobs" for you. Refer to my job evaluation table as a template.

Job Title and Duties	Is it a Good Job?
Doctor Deal with sick people all day. Try to help people who have abused their bodies for decades. Look at and touch all sorts of disgusting things. Make everyone wait at least an hour before seeing them.	Not for me.
Nurse Work with doctors to help patients recover. Care for the sick and elderly. Handle all kinds of bodily fluids.	Not for me.
Dentist Look at teeth and smell patients' foul breath all day.	Not for me.
Pharmacist Put pills in bottles and give to customers, keeping in mind that somebody could die if you goof up. Must memorize hundreds of drug names and their effects on the human body.	Not for me.

Job Title and Duties	Is it a Good Job?
Lawyer Read and write documents using language that no normal person can possibly understand.	Not for me.
Teacher Be around noisy kids all day. Must listen to obnoxious teenagers.	Two months off in summer is good. Otherwise, it's pure hell.
Police Officer Cruise around most of the time drinking coffee, but sometimes you must deal with violent sociopaths who try to kill you.	Not for me.
Firefighter Play cards most of the time, but sometimes you must fight a fire and risk your life because some drunken fool fell asleep with something on the stove, or some punk decided to light a building on fire.	Not for me.
Computer Professional Try to maintain computer hardware, software, and networks. Deal with nonstop network problems, glitches, security issues, hardware malfunctions, software bugs, and endless updates. Turn into a weirdo.	No thanks. My own computer frustrates me enough.

Job Title and Duties	Is it a Good Job?
Accountant Record and analyze financial information. Look at numbers, spreadsheets, and papers all day. Deal with taxation and regulations that are more complicated than anything in the universe.	The thought of it puts me to sleep.
Sales/Marketing Professional Visit customers, talk a lot about yourself, drink your face off, play golf, make promises that are impossible to keep, dress impeccably, and never get upset when customers shun you.	Sure, if you have no morals whatsoever.
Tradesperson (carpenter, electrician, plumber, etc.) Construct new buildings and/or renovate old buildings. Try to fix the previous work done by idiots. Crawl around on your hands and knees or on your back in dirty conditions trying to fix something that is fifty years old.	Not for me.
Airline Pilot Fly airplanes.	Sure, if you don't mind spending $100,000 for school to earn $25,000 per year to start.

Job Title and Duties	Is it a Good Job?
Truck Driver Drive trucks eighteen hours a day on congested roads through bad weather. Eat greasy food and suffer chronic health problems.	My ass is sore just thinking about it.
Engineer Go to meetings, answer emails, and get abused by the Sales department. Occasionally design something, making sure that simple things are redesigned to be more complicated. Try to design everything to be cheap and unfixable.	Not really. The work is usually difficult and stressful, and you always get blamed when things go wrong.
Mechanic Repair and maintain machines and vehicles. Get dirty and scrape knuckles. Curse and swear a lot about the moronic engineers who designed these pieces of sh*t.	Not for me.
Retail Sales Associate Stock shelves. Generally try to avoid customers, but sometimes a customer might catch you and ask a question that you don't know the answer to, so you have to make up something like, "It's in aisle eleven" or "We're sold out."	Not good unless you own the store.

Job Title and Duties	Is it a Good Job?
Factory Worker Fabricate and/or assemble products.	Everything will soon be made by robots or else made in China.
Robot Designer Design and build robots to replace factory workers.	The robots will also be made in China.
Food Services Worker Prepare meals and serve customers. Servers can earn good tips if they are attractive. Must work evenings and weekends to make any money.	Not bad in a high-end restaurant. Definitely not good in a fast-food joint.
Hotel Worker Front desk people deal with annoying travelers. Cleaning staff must clean rooms after drunken guests have engaged in all sorts of debauchery.	Are you kidding?
Social Worker, Therapist Try to help people with their problems.	I'm already helping you find a job. What more do you want?
Writer, Reporter, Journalist Investigate and write great works that few people will read.	Maybe, although you might have to live with your parents for most of your life.
Artist Create great works of art that nobody understands or cares about.	Maybe, if you have rich parents or a rich spouse.

Job Title and Duties	Is it a Good Job?
Musician, Actor, Entertainer Sing, dance, act, play a musical instrument, or tell jokes to entertain people. Pursue your passion and follow your dreams.	Perhaps, if it doesn't interfere with your waiter/waitress job.
Hair Stylist Cut hair. Successful ones must be able to fake interest in clients' personal lives and be able to carry on meaningless conversations all day.	Maybe, depending on how much you can pocket without paying taxes.
Social Media Influencer Post stupid photos and videos of yourself to attract brainless social media followers. Advertise crap. Get free stuff and money from advertisers.	It isn't a real job. However, you can make money if you are a complete narcissist.
Real Estate Agent Make obscene amounts of money selling overpriced houses and condos.	Sure, if you worship Satan.
Financial Planner Make tons of money peddling investments that you don't understand.	Sure, if you are Satan.
Government Worker Nobody knows what the duties are.	Maybe, if you can handle following dumb rules.

Job Title and Duties	Is it a Good Job?
Manager Go to meetings, write emails, walk around, chitchat with people, go out for lunch, and give instructions on topics you know nothing about. Thrive on chaos because it gives you something to do.	Perhaps, if you are bossy and egotistical and have Attention Deficit Disorder.
Coordinator Run around a lot with a piece of paper in your hand. Nobody knows what you do, but you always seem busy. Talk to everybody. Be highly visible.	Absolutely.
Analyst, Planner, Specialist, Researcher Sit at a desk in the corner working on a computer. Nobody knows what you do, but you always seem busy. Don't talk to a soul. Be invisible.	Absolutely.
Draftsperson Make drawings of machines or buildings. Work closely with engineers. Do similar work for half the salary.	I'd rather clean toilets.

Although virtually all drafting today is done on computers, the work of a draftsperson is still extremely detailed and tedious. In one of my stints as a mechanical draftsperson, I regularly worked late enough to encounter the cleaning person. One day while I was staring at my computer monitor, the cleaner asked me, "Do you have to look at that screen all day?"

I replied, "Yes, pretty much so."

He responded, "I would rather clean toilets."

To that I answered, "On many days, I would, too."

Let's review the job evaluation table. From my viewpoint, the best jobs are held by anyone with a job title that includes the word *analyst, planner, specialist, researcher,* or *coordinator.* To me, these are good jobs because their duties are completely ambiguous. In contrast, traditional jobs have clearly defined duties. If you say that you are a plumber, people automatically know what you do for a living. Your boss expects you to do plumbing. But if you say that you are a policy analyst or an administrative coordinator, nobody has a clue what you do. Your boss doesn't even know what you do. Therefore, you can do whatever you want with little stress and no deadlines yet get paid handsomely.

Remember, though, the preceding table contains **my** list of good jobs. Your list might be completely different from mine, and that's okay. You are perhaps energetic and idealistic, and you honestly want to make a difference in the world. You may have high standards and uncompromising principles. You may well be driven to succeed in the face of seemingly insurmountable challenges. If so, I applaud your zeal. I also think you need to slap yourself and get back to reality!

All right, you have now compiled a list of good jobs. Do you have the education, experience, or skills to qualify for any of them? If not, do you have the desire and financial resources available to acquire the education and skills needed to get one of your good jobs? Most people can't change course midstream. Once you have education and/or experience in one field, switching to something else is very difficult and expensive. So, if you can't ever land one of the good jobs from your list, was reading this chapter a complete waste of time? Probably.

Nevertheless, if you can't find a good job, which are rare, you should pursue a more common mediocre job. A mediocre job is better than a horrible job and certainly better than no job at all. Besides, in our modern world, mediocrity is the new normal. We want things fast and cheap. Nobody has time to do excellent work, and few people place much value on excellence anyway. Because our consumer marketplace is inundated with mediocre products and services, it should be no surprise that mediocre jobs have come to dominate the job market as well.

What Do You *Not* Want To Do?

Human Resources managers and recruiters regularly ask, "What do you want to do?" It's an easy question to answer if you actually know what you want to do. However, what if you don't know what you want to do? What if, like me, you don't want to do anything? You just want to stay home and do nothing. A much better question then would be, "What do you **not** want to do?"

If you are unsure of what you want to do, you should generate a list of tasks that you don't want to do in a job, such as in my list below:

List 1 - Things I Don't Want To Do
- Get dirty.
- Be uncomfortable.
- Lift heavy objects.
- Work in a high-stress environment.
- Do boring, dull, or monotonous work.
- Sit at a computer all day.
- Stand in one spot all day.
- Drive a vehicle all day.
- Answer phone calls, respond to emails, or go to meetings.
- Work with people.
- Start early in the morning.

Because no job on Earth fits this bill, I know I will be required to perform some objectionable duties in any job. The key is to set priorities for tasks that are unpleasant, and then try to minimize them in a job.

I do this by splitting my original list into two lists: *Things I Can Tolerate* (made up of tolerable tasks from my original list) and *Things I REALLY Don't Want To Do* (the revised list after I remove the tolerable tasks). Afterward, I have two lists as shown on the next page.

Revised List 1 - Things I REALLY Don't Want To Do
- Get dirty.
- Be uncomfortable.
- Lift heavy objects.
- Work in a high-stress environment.
- Stand in one spot all day.
- Drive a vehicle all day.

List 2 - Things I Can Tolerate
- Doing boring, dull, and monotonous work.
- Sitting at a computer all day.
- Answering phone calls, responding to emails, and going to meetings.
- Working with people.
- Starting early in the morning.

Now that I have two lists, I use them to evaluate potential job openings. I avoid jobs that have duties in the Revised List 1, but I consider jobs that have duties in List 2. When an interviewer asks me what I want to do, I pick one item from List 2 that best suits the job I am being interviewed for. For example, if I am applying for a job that primarily involves dealing with people, I tell the interviewer that I **love** working with people. If I am applying for a desk job, I tell the interviewer that I **love** sitting all day working in front of a computer. Both cases are a bit of a stretch, but I know either position would be acceptable to me. You will learn more about stretching the truth in a later chapter on job interviews.

By now, you are probably thinking, "Hey, I thought this guy said I wouldn't have to do any assignments in this book. What gives?"

Sorry, I tricked you. Do you honestly believe you can read a book about career planning and job hunting without needing to do some written exercises? Don't be so naive.

After making your lists, you should have a good idea of which jobs to pursue or to avoid. Remember, your goal is to find a decent job. By paying attention to the negative aspects of work, you can avoid horrible jobs and land more tolerable ones.

Be sure to include mediocre jobs in your job search because good jobs are scarce. Mediocre jobs can satisfy your monetary needs as well as your social needs. In my many years of working in mediocre jobs, I've met many good people (well, maybe not many, but at least three), and I've made some great friendships. Mediocre jobs also provide a good training ground because you often gain valuable knowledge and skills, which you can take along to future mediocre jobs.

You should also be aware that it is possible for any job to turn bad in an instant in today's fast-paced world. Today you may have a great boss, but tomorrow you might have a new boss who is a despicable tyrant. Work may go well today, but tomorrow you might inherit twice as much work because half of your department is getting laid off. These situations occur frequently and without warning. You can learn more about lay-off preparation in my next book (it's a cheap sales ploy, I know).

You are nearly ready to start exploring job-hunting techniques. But before you dive into job hunting, you should know a bit about business. You will likely be seeking employment with a private corporation, so having an overall understanding of business principles is vital. Once you understand the basics of business, you can better envision your role as a small cog in the machinery of industry. I promise you won't have to do any assignments in the next chapter.

2. Understanding Business

If you ever studied economics, you would have heard about the allocation of scarce resources, price elasticity, and other such gobbledygook. Well, forget that stuff. This chapter explains what you need to know about business.

Capitalism

Capitalism is an economic system in which two kinds of people exist:
1. People who have very little money and want more.
2. People who have a lot of money and want more.

From here on, the people with little money are referred to as the Regular Group, and the people with a lot of money are referred to as the Master Group. This system works as described in the rest of this chapter. Pay attention because, as a job hunter, you are in the Regular Group.

Regular Group people work for Master Group people, or else they work in government. Regular Group people purchase all of their products from the Master Group, borrow money from the Master Group, and even hand over their hard-earned savings to the Master Group in clever schemes called banking and mutual funds. You will learn more about such schemes later.

Regular Group people all envy Master Group people, but only a few Regular Group people are serious about trying to escape and joining the Master Group. These potential escapees are called "Entrepreneurs."

Entrepreneurs are the heart and soul of the capitalist system. Hard-working and creative, they are the ones who inspire change and innovation. Regular Group members cheer on the Entrepreneurs struggling to get into the Master Group, while Master Group members do everything possible to prevent Entrepreneurs from succeeding. Although most Entrepreneurs fail and end up staying in the Regular Group, some succeed and make it into the exclusive

Master Group. Once in the Master Group, the Entrepreneurs usually turn into a**holes.

The goal of the capitalist system is to make money without doing any real work. Regular Group members try to do this by buying lottery tickets and gambling in casinos. Master Group members do it by investing and speculating. Regular Group people seldom succeed and must continue to do all the unpleasant work in the world, whereas Master Group people let their money do their work for them while they enjoy luxurious lifestyles. Master Group members keep busy managing their hoards of money, which they strangely call "work."

Busy-ness

Most jobs in society are not a whole lot of fun, such as cleaning toilets and working in factories. Regular Group people are busy all day performing these types of jobs. Their jobs, as unpleasant as they often are, typically have tangible results. For example, if you see a gravel road at the start of the day and a paved road at the end of the day, rest assured Regular Group people did the work.

Master Group people, on the other hand, don't need to work because their money is working. Nevertheless, they are bored if they aren't busy, so they invent jobs and entire industries (financial services, wealth management, etc.) to keep them busy. These jobs are fluffy jobs, which don't create anything much of lasting value. For example, you might see a bunch of numbers in one column at the start of the day, and you might see a bunch of numbers in another column at the end of the day. Big deal. But it is a big deal for Master Group people because, in some mysterious way,

Master Group people make a lot of money by having those numbers move around. The next day the numbers could be back in the first column, and once again, some Master Group people will make money. Think about that the next time you are cleaning somebody's toilet or working on an assembly line in a sweltering hot factory.

The term "business" is coined from the busy work of the Master Group. (Busy + Ness = Business).

Banking

Banking is a two-part system involving deposits and credit. Centuries ago, charging interest was considered a sin in most religions. As a result, few people were willing to lend money. The exception was with people of Jewish faith, who could lend money and charge interest to non-Jews. A few wealthy Christians wanted in on the action, so they figured out how to get around the sin by charging "commissions" instead of "interest." That was good enough for the Pope, and modern banking was born.

At the same time, people needed a secure place to store money, so they started to deposit their savings into the banks' vaults. The bankers then had some customers who wanted loans and other customers who wanted a safe place to store their money. The bankers saw all these deposits of money sitting idly in their vaults and thought, "Why don't we pretend this is our money and lend it out?"

And that's exactly what they did. The bankers kept a small percentage of deposits in their vaults in case an occasional customer wanted to take some money out (called fractional reserve banking). The rest of the money was lent out. The bankers paid depositors a pittance, charged borrowers a much higher rate, and pocketed the difference. It was pure genius.

The plan's success was based on faith. As long as depositors believed that they could withdraw their money at any time, they were happy, and as long as bankers believed that borrowers would pay back their loans, bankers were happy.

The system had an inherent problem, though. When borrowers failed to pay their debts (called loan defaults), a bank lost money. But the money lost was not the bank's money; it was the depositors' money. Oops! After depositors heard the news about defaults, they all tried to withdraw their funds at the same time (called a run on the bank). Only a few people, however, were able to retrieve their money, and most came out empty handed. Subsequently, mobs of angry depositors often rioted and lynched the bankers.

Bankers realized early on that they could reduce their risk of being lynched by having large banks with many depositors. Today we have huge banking institutions that manage billions of dollars and earn outrageous profits by paying depositors .1% interest while charging borrowers 20% interest on credit cards. Bankers are no longer lynched for making bad loans but instead bailed out by the government and paid bonuses.

Marketing

Marketing is the action of convincing people to buy things they don't need. It is an essential part of our modern economy. Let's face it. If we only bought what we really needed, the economy would slow to a crawl, and unemployment would hover around 80%. Because of marketing, we have a reasonably strong global economy with millions of people working diligently producing and transporting stuff we don't need.

Marketing has completely transformed our world. One hundred and fifty years ago, most people lived in squalor and labored long hours just to provide the necessities of life—food, shelter, and clothing. A luxury was a hot bath, a piece of candy, or being able to stand beside a person who didn't smell of sweat and manure. It was a hard life.

Today we still work long hours, but the definition of necessity has changed significantly because of good marketing. A necessity today is a 3000 sq. ft. house with four bedrooms, three bathrooms, and an open concept kitchen with granite countertops. Driving a fully loaded SUV is now a necessity because we might encounter an inch of snow while driving in the city, or we might get the urge to drive to the top of a mountain. Smartphones are an absolute necessity in today's world because we need to be in constant communication with our loser friends and helpless family members. An annual vacation to an exotic location is a necessity because we work so hard and deserve some time to relax. And let's not forget that going out to restaurants regularly is now a necessity because, well, we have to eat!

Marketing is also responsible for the fact we have 14,000 different hair care products on the supermarket shelves and 600 different brands of toothpaste. When I used to go shopping a few decades ago, there were two different brands of toothpaste. Either one suited me just fine. I could pick one out in five seconds and be on my way. Today I must walk down a 50-yard-long aisle filled with hundreds of different brands of toothpaste. With all these choices, trying to decide is excruciating. Should I buy toothpaste with tartar control, whitening, tartar control PLUS whitening, cavity prevention, or added fresh breath? It now takes twenty minutes to buy toothpaste. Thank you, Marketing!

Marketers always justify their actions by claiming they are simply responding to customer demand. They imply that hordes of irate customers are picketing outside the factories demanding that the company produces a new brand of toothpaste specific to this group's needs. In reality, marketers are workaholics who can't sit still. They need to keep busy, so when they aren't drinking or playing golf, they dream up new products and services.

They do have strict guidelines, however, to evaluate which ideas to pursue. Before launching a new product, all proposals are carefully scrutinized by asking two fundamental questions:
1. Is the new product useful, safe, and environmental?
2. Can the company make money from it?

If they answer "yes" to question #2, they ignore question #1, and work commences immediately with a sense of urgency similar to a military campaign. A product development team of engineers, technicians, chemists, programmers, and many others work feverishly to introduce this new product into the market in the fastest time possible. Meanwhile, the Marketing gurus drink, play golf, and discuss more ideas for new products and services. They are the catalyst that keeps the entire economic system churning.

Advertising is another important function of Marketing. It's not enough that Marketing gives us thousands of nearly identical products; they must also inform us about the tremendous benefits these products offer. Therefore, in case people aren't fat and unhealthy enough, extensive advertising is conducted to promote the newest pizza or burger, which is so much tastier than previous versions. Also, in case we might forget about the top-selling brands of pizza, burgers, tampons, cars, beer, soap, or whatever, advertisers make sure we see ads on TV every few minutes, repeated over and over again until a one-hour-long football game becomes four hours long. In addition, we are bombarded with non-stop animated ads on websites, we see ads before we can watch an online video, and we see ads on every second page of a magazine. Once again, thank you, Marketing!

Advertisers understand perfectly well that adults behave much the same way as children do. If a colorful, interesting object is waved in front of a baby's face, the baby immediately reaches up to grab the item. If the baby can't grab hold of it, he or she starts to cry. But if the baby is able to grab hold of the item, he or she looks at it, chews on it, plays with it for a minute, and then throws it on the floor.

Most adults react in a similar manner. If advertisers flash a shiny, new object in front of us, we want it, and we are unhappy if we can't have it. Once we do obtain it, though, we usually use it for a few minutes and then hide it in a closet for a few years before eventually throwing it away. Also, like children, we always desire things that are bad for us. Children never turn down ice cream or candy, but they habitually turn their noses up when offered carrots or broccoli. Likewise, adults buying cars can seldom turn down vehicles with 300 horsepower, leather interior, alloy wheels, and built-in navigation. But we turn up our noses when offered reliable, economical subcompacts.

Advertisers are masters of creating fantasy. We see ads on TV featuring shiny cars with beautiful occupants driving along scenic roads with no other cars in sight. But when I'm driving my car in the real world, I am normally surrounded by cars and big trucks and traveling over vast stretches of pothole-ravaged roads. There is nothing beautiful about it. Similarly, TV ads show gorgeous, sexy women wolfing down bacon double cheeseburgers. I can't remember observing that in real life, either. I guess I should eat fast food more often.

To ensure that companies have an endless stream of repeat customers, Marketers employ stylists and various designers (industrial designers, fashion designers, interior designers, etc.), depending on the industry. The job of stylists and designers is to make sure that anything purchased today looks like crap in two years. An item may function properly for many years (highly unlikely with today's products), but it is absolutely imperative that the item looks tired, worn, dated, out of style, and just plain ugly in a short period of time.

No matter how much is spent on a perceived high-quality product today, a consumer must always feel the need to update his or her clothes, furniture, appliances, home, electronic devices, and automobile within a short time span. The goal is to ensure that customer satisfaction is fleeting and short lived.

If black is the current "in" color, stylists and designers use a different color in all their new designs, such as silver. Consumers, seeing that their black products are out of style, crave the new silver ones, which are prominently displayed everywhere from an extensive advertising blitz. Eventually consumers cave into temptation and replace all their black possessions with silver. After two years, when nearly everyone has switched to silver, stylists and designers will introduce black as a "retro" look. Once again, consumers will feel compelled to replace their belongings, this time replacing the silver with black. These good marketing techniques create a virtual perpetual motion machine of selling and spending.

Gross Domestic Product (GDP)

Gross Domestic Product (GDP) is a measurement of the monetary value of all goods and services produced in a country in a particular period. Economists and politicians place a great deal of importance on GDP growth. However, GDP is a rather flawed measurement because it is based on monetary transactions, not on the usefulness of the actual work accomplished.

For example, if you had grown some vegetables in your back yard and made a salad, you would not have contributed to GDP because no money was exchanged. It doesn't matter that you worked hard. On the other hand, if you had purchased the vegetables from a supermarket and made a salad, a financial transaction would have occurred, and GDP would have increased. Moreover, if you had simply gone to a restaurant and ordered a salad, GDP would have increased even more.

Not all intermediate transactions are counted in the GDP calculation, but if jobs are created, the nation's economy is better off. A modern family that eats out every meal and pays for babysitting, daycare, cleaning, laundry, and household repairs is contributing significantly to economic growth. Therefore, they are very patriotic. They are even more patriotic if they are up to their eyeballs in debt living paycheck to paycheck. In contrast, a family that looks after their own kids, cooks their own meals, does their own household chores, and has no credit card debt is rather anti-capitalistic, which basically makes them communists.

Trickle Down Economics

Trickle Down Economics is the theory that extra money made by the Master Group eventually trickles down to the Regular Group. The thinking is that if a king is fed so much food that he can't eat all of it, he will leave a few more scraps for the starving masses. For obvious reasons, the theory is extremely popular with the wealthy.

Proponents of the theory encourage governments to lower taxes on the rich to promote economic growth and hiring. For example, if the government cut taxes on a rich person by $500,000, the rich person might buy a boat (made overseas), and then hire someone for $10/hour ($20,000/year) to clean and maintain the new boat. The economy benefits because the newly hired cleaner spends his or her salary, and the boat owner spends more as well (fuel for the boat from offshore oil and imported wine for parties on the boat).

The newly hired person also pays taxes ($3000/year). The government ends up $497,000 worse off, so they need to borrow more money (sell more bonds), which increases the national debt. However, the government has two more voters (the boat owner and the person hired). For obvious reasons, the theory is extremely popular with wealthy politicians.

Corporations and the Stock Market

Up until a few hundred years ago, commercial enterprises were mainly sole proprietorships and partnerships. Both types of businesses functioned well and still do today. Nonetheless, both are limited in their potential size and the amount of capital they can raise.

With the onset of colonialism and industrialism, private enterprises had a strong desire to exploit more people and pillage more resources around the globe. Traditionally, the armies of monarchs and empires carried out the looting of new territories. But by the 17th century, businesspeople wanted in on the raiding, too. To fulfill this desire for expansion required raising large amounts of capital. Thus, a new type of venture was invented—the corporation. Groups of people pooled their money and became stockholders (also called shareholders) in these new corporations.

To encourage people to invest, laws were implemented that allowed corporations to be recognized as singular entities with the same rights as individuals. The concept of limited liability was introduced. Unlike partnerships, in which each partner is responsible for the debts of the others, corporations have limited liability, in which no individual shareholder is responsible for the debts of the others. The most money a shareholder can lose is his or her original investment. Profits of a corporation are distributed to its shareholders via dividends.

Initially, the buying and selling of a corporation's shares was closed to the public. Therefore, a corporation was constrained in the size it could grow to because of its small number of shareholders and the lack of liquidity of its stock. To become a true global plunderer, a corporation required thousands of shareholders to invest.

To attract shareholders from the general public required more liquid stock because most people would not invest unless they could convert their shares to cash quickly and easily. A corporation would seldom buy back its shares because it needed the cash for its own expansion. Getting cash from investors was the whole idea for becoming a corporation in the first place. (Buying back shares is common today because corporations are flush with cash, and they would rather buy back shares to keep stock prices inflated rather than expand or hire workers.)

The solution to this problem was the emergence of the stock exchange. It is a secondary market where existing shareholders can sell their shares for cash to traders, who in turn sell the shares to other buyers in the public. A corporation that wants to exchange its shares in this way lists its stock on a stock exchange. Such a corporation is called a public corporation.

The term public corporation is a bit deceiving. Although the buying and selling of shares is technically open to the public, the process involves financial experts like brokers, traders, dealers, and investment bankers to be involved. This makes the stock market a perfect environment for swindlers.

Also interesting is the notion that a public corporation owned by private citizens is the embodiment of the free enterprise capitalistic system, but a public corporation owned by the government (owned by the actual public) is considered socialism and is pure evil.

The stock market is somewhat like the used-car market, except that used-car salespeople are generally more trustworthy than people on Wall Street. The used-car market has no direct effect on the bottom line of car manufacturers because they make money selling new cars. Likewise, the stock market has no direct effect on the finances of a public corporation because the cash is accounted for when the shares are originally sold.

One noteworthy difference between the two markets (aside from rapid depreciation of automobiles versus long-term life of stocks) is that used cars are frequently fixed up before selling, creating an element of added value. Some actual work goes into the profits, whereas no real work is done to earn stock market profits. The shares going in are exactly the same as the ones coming out. The only work done is the "work" of those involved in the transaction. The stock market, then, is the ultimate way to make money without doing any real work, which explains its popularity and importance to the Master Group people in our modern economy.

Although the share price has no direct effect on a public corporation's finances, the share price fluctuations affect the decisions made by the senior managers because they report to the shareholders, and senior managers are often compensated based on the share price. Shareholders are always comparing the market value of their shares against the price they paid for them. If the share price goes up, shareholders are happy and optimistic, and they assume more risk. Conversely, if the share price falls, they are unhappy, pessimistic, and cautious. Shareholders may even sell their shares in a panic that causes the share price to fall further. This roller coaster of share prices and shareholder emotions influences the decisions of executives in managing their corporations. Decisions of executives to expand business or cut costs affect the number of jobs gained or lost. Consequently, the stock market and the number of jobs in the economy are highly affected by the emotions of a small group of hyperactive, paranoid people.

In addition to the stock markets, we have the bond markets, currency markets, futures markets, commodities markets, etc., which are lumped together in a term called "the markets." These markets are the epitome of busy-ness with brash traders buying and selling by the minute in a frenzy of activity. Short-term speculation has replaced long-term investment as billions of dollars move around each day without creating anything of real value. An amazing system has developed in which enormous wealth can be generated without producing any goods or useful services, except the service provided to generate more wealth. Like watching a magician making objects appear out of thin air, we are fascinated by "the markets." Comparable to a magician's act, though, wealth in the markets can vanish in a moment, too. These magicians manage our entire financial system, which is a somewhat frightening thought.

Supply and Demand

One of the fundamental theories in economics is supply and demand theory, which is mostly common sense. If demand exceeds supply, prices go up. If supply exceeds demand, prices should fall. Economists use graphs to show supply and demand curves, and a theoretical price equilibrium point exists where the curves intersect. Various factors affect the slopes of the curves and blah, blah, blah...you get the idea.

In the real world, prices typically go up as soon as demand exceeds supply, such as with hotel rooms, concert tickets, and illegal drugs (I wouldn't know, but that's what I've been told). Yet prices don't always come down even if an abundant supply exists. Many industries are controlled by a few large corporations that all charge the same prices for their products. Only several conglomerates produce the 14,000 hair-care products mentioned earlier. They control the supply and set the prices accordingly.

Prior to the COVID-19 pandemic, our modern economy had ample capacity to supply all the goods we needed. Our productive high-tech factories and farms ensured a plentiful supply of virtually every product imaginable. Our store shelves were overflowing with consumer products and car dealers' lots were packed with new cars. Shortages were practically unheard of in the global free-market economy. We are presently experiencing some supply chain problems due to the pandemic, but these problems are temporary, and the supply of goods will undoubtedly return to normal after the pandemic recedes.

To find buyers for all these products, corporations continually need to increase demand. They do this with clever marketing and advertising and by offering credit. Without credit purchases, the economy collapses. Business and governments require consumers to spend more than they earn to keep the system afloat. What happens in the future is not a concern. Of primary importance to business and governments is to ensure that the economy keeps growing, no matter what. Workers, who are also consumers, rely on this growth to create the jobs needed to provide income necessary to buy more of this unneeded stuff.

Can't you work faster? Our customers need more stuff!

3. The Search Is On

The Job Market

Now that you have a good knowledge of business principles, you should be better able to understand some of the realities of today's job market. The number of job opportunities you encounter and the wages you are paid are determined by the laws of supply and demand. Working hard and being useful to society are quite irrelevant in the job market, as evidenced by the fact that many talented, hard-working people employed in noble occupations earn very little. In today's world, a software developer who creates super-violent video games is paid much more than a teacher, who arguably has one of the most important jobs in society. A financial trader who gambles on stocks to earn money for a rich client earns more than a doctor who saves lives. These apparent injustices are easily explained in a market-driven economy. You see, your value in the job market depends on how much money an employer can make from using your services (demand side) in relation to the number of people available who can deliver those services (supply side).

An abundant supply of workers exists in a majority of occupations today, except for various highly skilled professions. When the demand for these workers exceeds the supply, post-secondary schools respond by creating programs to increase the supply of graduates. Unfortunately, by the time graduates enter the job market, circumstances may have changed and a surplus might occur. In my lifetime, I have witnessed shortages and surpluses of nurses, teachers, engineers, and tradespeople.

The supply of some occupations is managed by professional associations that continually make it more difficult to be accredited so exorbitant salaries can be maintained for those in the field (such as lawyers and public accountants). Other occupations are competitive on a global scale, as companies either import workers to fill skill shortages (shortages that are mainly the result of companies' unwillingness to train people) or outsource the work to foreign countries (like many IT jobs). It is difficult enough to compete against local job hunters, but nowadays you might also compete indirectly against job hunters in other nations.

A major characteristic of today's job market is the plague of underemployment, as many people presently work in jobs much below their education and skill level. We have the most educated population in history, yet the bulk of the jobs created in the past few decades are menial, low-skilled jobs. Consequently, university-educated people compete with non-degree holders for the same low-paying jobs.

Business and government fuel the demand for workers. Governments everywhere, though, are under intense pressure to control spending because of enormous debts. As a result, the demand for workers in government is flat. Businesses, large and small, are the engines for job creation now and in the foreseeable future. However, the business community, despite strong sales, has a low demand for workers in many industries because of the increasing use of technology and outsourcing.

Because of technological advancements and increased importation, fewer workers are needed to produce all the goods we require. According to statistics, about 9% of the workforce is employed in manufacturing, and about 4% work on farms. Therefore, demand for workers in manufacturing and agriculture is declining, except for a few highly specialized occupations. Because it takes only 13% of the workforce to supply all the food and manufactured products we need, what do the other 87% do? They predominantly work in services. (I estimate 50% are telemarketers, 35% are writers of job-hunting books, and 2% do everything else.)

A number of these service jobs are essential (e.g., medical occupations, utility workers, and police). Life would certainly be difficult without people performing these jobs. Most of us do not want to live without electricity, running water, doctors, or police. We have few alternatives to using these services because we can't perform the jobs ourselves (some people try, but they have limited success).

On the other hand, many of the jobs created in recent decades are quite unnecessary to society as a whole (e.g., telemarketers, recruiters, advertisers, real estate agents, financial planners, and pet groomers). We can manage without their services because other alternatives exist. We can do the work ourselves if necessary, or as in the case of telemarketing and advertising, we can find other ways to become annoyed and irritated.

Many new jobs are in businesses that serve niche markets with somewhat frivolous services that primarily cater to the wealthy. Another growing segment is the service of providing entertainment to a generally apathetic public. Your best chance of employment, therefore, will be with companies that provide non-essential services. By providing relatively useless, time-wasting activities for society, you can earn much more than by trying to do good things for humanity.

The business community may have a steady demand for workers but not necessarily a demand for you as an individual. You see, workers are a commodity to business, with one employee being nearly indistinguishable from another. To find a job, you need to differentiate yourself from your competitors, which are plentiful in most occupations today. You need to utilize marketing to convince a prospective employer to hire you instead of one of your competitors.

Like marketing any other product or service, you must think of companies as customers who don't really know what they want. They have money, however, and you want some of it. With good marketing, you can convince a company to give you money in exchange for your perceived superior abilities. Although you may be competing against hundreds of people for the coveted mediocre jobs, you have a distinct advantage because you are one of the few people who are actually reading my book. In the next few chapters, you will learn some proven techniques to sell yourself to prospective employers.

The Waiting Game

Decades ago, looking for a job was much simpler than today. The typical hiring process fifty years ago would go something like this:

1. A job hunter would approach a local business and ask someone directly if there were any job openings.
2. If the business had no openings, the job hunter was usually told immediately, "Sorry, we are not hiring right now." The job seeker would stroke this company off his or her list and continue searching.
3. If the business had job openings, interviews often were conducted on the spot, and people were hired immediately. Sometimes the job seeker was asked to fill out an application. Applications were reviewed quickly, and interviews were conducted soon after. Suitable workers were hired within days. Neither job seekers nor employers were overly picky.

Compare that to the modern job search:
1. You spend weeks preparing your resume. You read dozens of

online articles and books written by HR people for help.
2. You spend countless hours scrolling through hundreds of jobs listed on job-search websites. You find a few jobs that are of interest, but many of them are from agencies, which don't provide actual company names or locations (the job might be across town from where you live). You have no idea of the salaries for most of the jobs. You submit resumes anyway.
3. You look at corporate websites of companies in your field. Most sites have a Careers page that lists current job openings and contact info. You apply for interesting positions and send unsolicited resumes and cover letters to HR departments.
4. You wait.
5. After waiting for several weeks, one of the companies that you contacted calls you. You are asked to come in for an interview. You spend hours or days preparing for the job interview.
6. You have an interview with an HR person who asks many inane questions like, "Where do you see yourself in five years?" and "Describe your ideal job." After a grueling interview, you are asked what your salary expectations are, or they may tell you what the salary range is. If the interview is with an employment agency, you learn that the job is with company XYZ (probably located on the other side of the city, guaranteeing a long, horrible commute if you get the job).
7. You wait.

After several weeks of waiting, you generally hear nothing back from the company. In many cases, you are not surprised because the interview went terribly. However, sometimes you are baffled as to why you didn't hear back because you thought the interview went well. Were you asking for too much money? Did they find someone with better credentials or more experience? You will never know.

In some situations, you had no chance of getting the job. The position might have been filled by a person with connections to the inside of the organization, and interviews were only conducted to satisfy an internal policy. Other times, the position was never filled because of changing circumstances (e.g., budget cuts, project cancellation, or corporate restructuring). In any case, the interview was a waste of time.

After a lengthy wait, you could be called in for a second interview. On rare occasions, you might even receive a job offer after the first interview. Nevertheless, by the time you receive the call, you are often onto another job prospect.

As you can see, to receive a job offer usually requires you to go through the many steps shown. The elapsed time is weeks, maybe even months, before you learn whether your job application was successful or not. Companies sometimes spend months recruiting for people to fill temporary positions. Even minimum wage job seekers today are regularly forced to go through this lengthy process.

Networking

To avoid the time-consuming, complicated steps required to find a job in the electronic age, many job seekers utilize something called networking. Networking is a modern term for an old-school method—find work by word of mouth. Simply ask people you know if they are aware of any suitable job openings.

For generations, the most predominant way people found jobs was through word of mouth. A friend works for a company that is hiring and recommends you for the job. An uncle has a neighbor who owns a business that could use your services, and your uncle puts in a good word for you.

Bypassing the formal system benefits both the job hunter and the employer. The employer benefits by saving the time of looking through hundreds of resumes and conducting multiple interviews. In addition, the employer's risk is lessened by having a trusted employee vouch for the prospective new employee. The job hunter's risk is also lessened by having a trusted friend or relative on the inside who already knows the corporate culture and personalities of managers and other workers.

I encourage you to use networking as much as possible, particularly if you are seeking employment in motorcycle gangs or organized crime syndicates. Such organizations rarely post job ads, so networking is your best avenue for finding work in these groups.

The more people you have in your networking circle, the greater your odds of success in finding a job. There is one exception, though. If you happen to be a totally useless worker, few of your contacts will recommend you. In that case, the more people you know, the worse your chances of landing a job because word gets around. In situations like that, it is best **not** to know people on the inside because they will discourage their bosses from hiring you. To find a job, you might have to move to a city where nobody knows you.

Resumes

The first step in marketing yourself is to produce a quality resume, which is simply a written summary of your education, work experience, and job qualifications. Even if you use networking in your job search, you still need to create a resume to send to your contacts. The exception is with violent, street-level criminals, who should not record their accomplishments in a resume (e.g., 5 years of experience as a thug, wacked 2 guys, pulled off 12 successful heists). However, non-violent thieves such as lawyers and financial advisers typically require professional resumes, as do blue-collar criminals such as contractors in the home-renovation industry.

Thousands of books and online articles offer advice in creating resumes. Unfortunately, this ocean of information contains a number of opposing opinions. Some writers believe that a resume should include an objective, but others declare that this statement is obsolete. Some "experts" recommend that a resume not exceed one page in length, whereas others suggest two pages. Some advocate that the work history does not go back more than ten years, but others say fifteen to twenty years is acceptable. No wonder the average person is perplexed when attempting to put together a resume.

To add to the confusion, many writers on the topic suggest that resumes should focus on accomplishments, not just descriptions of previous job duties. That's fine for a manager who might have accomplishments like:
- Increased sales by 20% in one year.

- Implemented a cost reduction program that saved $1.25 million in the first year.

(In actuality, executives accomplish little by themselves. Most achievements in business and government require the efforts of many people, but senior managers frequently accept credit for successes and blame others for failures.)

For a typical worker, though, accomplishments are relatively unglamorous:
- Did stuff my boss asked me to do.
- Re-did stuff my boss asked me to do because he always changed his mind.
- Finished projects my co-workers started because they were yanked off to work on other urgent, critical assignments.
- Refrained from punching the people who irritated me.

Such real-life achievements rarely look inspiring on a resume. Therefore, if you are unable to list any true accomplishments in your career, just spice up your mundane, meaningless tasks to look more impressive. Try to show that you are a person of action who gets things done by starting sentences with powerful verbs like:

advised	aided	analyzed
assembled	assisted	built
communicated	coordinated	created
delivered	demonstrated	designed
developed	directed	distributed
facilitated	formed	guided
handled	helped	implemented
initiated	installed	investigated

maintained	managed	modified
negotiated	operated	organized
planned	prepared	presented
produced	provided	repaired
served	set up	supervised
supplied	transported	utilized

For example, if you spent most of your time on the job talking about sports with your co-workers, you could say:
- Communicated extensively with project team members to develop system specifications.

If one of your main functions was to bring coffee and doughnuts to your boss and others in meetings, you could say:
- Distributed key components to management for development of strategic plans.
- Coordinated with vendors to supply critical resources in a Just-In-Time environment.

If you spent a lot of time at work selling raffle tickets for your kid's school, you could say:
- Initiated sales activities to generate additional finances.

If you sold more tickets this year than last year, you could also add:
- Growth of funds exceeded 20% on a year-to-year basis.

After you have compiled a list of your job duties and "accomplishments" and made them look impressive, you need to combine this flowery, fluffy drivel together with any real skills and truly valuable experience you may have. Your resume needs to impress both the HR department and the department manager who actually has a need for your services.

The HR department's job is to screen out most of the resumes and then forward a select few to the managers who have open positions in their departments. The HR personnel usually have little understanding of the technical aspects of most jobs in their organizations. Consequently, they relate more to the "fluff" (vague accomplishments and self-professed people skills) of an applicant's resume than the "meat" (real skills, actual knowledge, and relevant experience). As a result, many qualified people are overlooked because their resumes don't impress the HR department in the thirty seconds allocated to looking over a typical resume.

The department managers normally are more interested in a resume's substance or "meat" because they want to find candidates who are best suited to doing the actual work. If you are a machinist looking for a job, the machine shop supervisor doesn't care that your resume has a profile that states you are a results-oriented team player. The supervisor wants to know if you can operate a lathe and a milling machine. Your resume, therefore, must have some substance to warrant consideration by a department manager. However, if you exaggerate your skills and knowledge relating to main areas of the job, your shortcomings will be exposed quickly should you be interviewed or hired.

Unfortunately, the tendency of department managers to understand job details is changing because many managers in the modern world lack technical expertise and are totally inept when it comes to doing any real work. These managers are completely clued out about the actual skills required in their own departments and are as equally impressed with "fluff" as the HR department. In addition, the incompetent department managers are often insecure and easily intimidated by applicants who are too knowledgeable or too experienced. As a result, the bungling managers who actually have the power to hire overlook many qualified people.

I formerly worked as a mechanical draftsperson for a large manufacturer. One of my co-workers, Kelly, was generally lost when it came to using the Computer Aided Design (CAD) software. Kelly struggled and made many mistakes.

I learned one day that Kelly was actually a scientist who had no mechanical design or CAD experience. The company's management was impressed with Kelly's degree and thought it would be beneficial, even though Kelly's education had no relevance to the job.

As you can see, it will be extremely difficult to get your resume past the HR screening process and then considered by department managers, many of which are scatterbrains. Nevertheless, you can increase your chances of success by paying attention to the following points:

- Make sure your resume is professional looking. Numerous examples of resumes are available online. Find a sample you like and follow that structure.
- Ensure your resume has absolutely no spelling mistakes.
- Don't worry too much about the formatting. Many online submittal systems remove the formatting anyway and convert

resumes to plain text. Some people suggest not using tables or headers/footers because it might confuse the HR screening software.
- Keep your resume as brief as possible. I can condense 20+ years of work experience onto a one-page resume, so you should be able to as well. Use two pages if you have a lot of relevant experience.
- Use bullet points and short sentences to list your education, skills, relevant experience, and "accomplishments."
- Only list the jobs that will help in your job search. Don't mention ones that lasted only a few months unless they are relevant to the position you are applying for.

Many resume-writing experts suggest including a profile or summary section at the top of a resume. It seems redundant because the same information is listed elsewhere, but it's a good idea. A typical resume is viewed for only a few seconds, so having the highlights easily viewed will increase your chances of being noticed.

Some resume samples also have an "Objective" section at the top with some lame objective such as, "To find a challenging and rewarding position in Marketing with a progressive firm." In reality, the majority of us have an objective that is better stated as, "To find an easy job that pays well." Don't bother writing your objective. By applying for a specific job, the objective is implied. If you send an unsolicited resume to a company, include a short email message (today's version of cover letter) that describes the type of job you are looking for.

By providing job dates in years only, you can more easily leave off irrelevant jobs. You can also make short duration jobs appear longer. For example, if you started a job in December 2014 and quit a month later in January 2015, you could show it on your resume as:

Company ABC   2014-2015

That way it looks as if you worked at the company for a year instead of a month.

I prefer having the date on the same row as the Company with the position titles below. It looks better in case multiple positions were held in the same company.

Company XYZ   2010-2013
Production Coordinator
- *Coordinated...blah, blah, blah*

Planning Analyst
- *Planned...blah, blah, blah*
- *Analyzed...blah, blah, blah*

In this way, I can disguise the fact that I spent only three months as a Planning Analyst. I can also hide the fact that I left the company in 2011 for another job that didn't work out and then returned in 2012 to my old job. The job in between is forgotten and never needs to be mentioned.

Some sample resumes include an ending sentence, "References supplied on request." Again, don't waste space on this line. If companies want your references, they will ask for them in an interview. Everyone knows that you will ask three of your current or former co-workers to be references and to give rave reviews about you. Your references aren't going to say anything bad; otherwise, you wouldn't ask them to be references. If you are going to include a line at the bottom about references, you might as well say, "Bogus references supplied on request."

You don't have to limit yourself to one resume. Depending on your occupation and experience, you may need to have several resumes. In fact, you may need to have a different resume to suit each job that you apply for. If you have a lot of varied experience, you should try to match your resume to the qualifications sought after in a job posting, making sure to include the keywords that are listed in the ad. Highlight your relevant skills and experience while leaving off unrelated skills and experience. It's a lot of extra work, I know, but this is the reality of modern job hunting. Make sure you are organized so you can locate the appropriate version in case you are called in for an interview. Pulling out the wrong resume in an interview is highly embarrassing.

Most HR professionals recommend omitting personal hobbies and interests from resumes. However, if you have an interesting hobby that might be shared by a hiring manager, it could be a benefit to include it on your resume.

Earlier in my career, I was involved with reviewing resumes for a new position in our department. One applicant's resume stated his hobby was restoring old cars. My supervisor, who liked old cars, was impressed and selected that person for an interview primarily because of their shared interest.

Although omissions and embellishments on your resume are quite acceptable, don't outright lie or make absurd false statements unless you are trying to be elected as a state or federal politician.

Cover Letters

Even though the formal cover letter is somewhat obsolete in the electronic age, sending a short electronic cover message along with your resume is a good idea. If you are applying for an advertised position, the message should contain a couple of paragraphs to briefly explain why you are qualified for the job. If the company is large, however, they may use software to screen resumes, and no one will read your cover letter anyway.

If you are sending an unsolicited resume that has no stated objective, a cover message quickly lets the HR department know what kind of job you are seeking. Otherwise, the recipient does not know what kind of job you are looking for. Are you seeking a position as a software developer, an accountant, an engineer, or a maintenance worker? Without a cover message, your unsolicited resume probably won't go far (as far as the trash bin, perhaps).

The Launch

Now that you have your resume(s) ready to go, what's next? You must send off your masterpiece to companies that are dying to hear from you. Your phone will be ringing off the hook in no time, right?

I am sorry to disappoint you. Even with a good resume, the odds are stacked against you because of the overwhelming volume of resumes floating around cyberspace and sitting on computer servers.

In the electronic age, distributing resumes has become too easy and too cheap. When job hunters had to mail resumes or drop them off in person, the cost and inconvenience made job seekers more selective. Job hunters now can fire off dozens of resumes in a day from the comfort of their homes at no cost. Companies in the past had to place expensive ads in newspapers, whereas companies today can simply place ads on their website at low cost. As a result, companies are flooded with resumes, and many qualified applicants are turned away.

In today's world, the resume of Leonardo da Vinci or Albert Einstein would likely end up in the trash bin of most companies. But don't let that knowledge discourage you. Those guys were eccentrics who mainly worked alone. Unlike you, neither da Vinci nor Einstein was a team player who thrived in a fast-paced environment. How do I know you are a team player who thrives in a fast-paced environment? Well, your resume says so, of course!

Your principal job search tool will undoubtedly be the internet. Social networking sites like LinkedIn are immensely popular and can be useful in obtaining job leads. In addition, job search sites like Indeed, Monster, and Workopolis post thousands of positions. There are also government job banks and local websites that list job openings.

You should also research companies that interest you and send unsolicited resumes. If you happen to have the right qualifications and approach them at the right time, you might get a job opportunity without having the extensive competition that comes with applying for advertised positions. A small or medium-sized company may not have an official job opening for you, but they could be so impressed with your resume that they might consider creating a new position for you.

Another possibility is that the company has a new job opening yet to be advertised. If you come onto the scene at this time, you have a tremendous head start on your competition. The company might not even bother advertising. Instead, you could be interviewed and subsequently hired without having to go through any formal competition.

Still, if a company is struggling financially or if a company is managing fine with their current staff, they will have no openings regardless of how qualified you are. They are unlikely to fire a current employee to make room for you, although it has been known to happen.

I previously worked for a company whose general manager was a severe alcoholic. One day the GM was drinking in his office with one of the employees, Dan, and the GM asked Dan to consider becoming the plant supervisor. Dan was hesitant in responding because the company already had a plant supervisor, Jerry. Before Dan could answer, the GM said, "While you're thinking about it, I'm going to go fire Jerry."

The GM fired Jerry and then came back a few minutes later to hear Dan's answer. Dan reluctantly agreed to be the new plant supervisor, even though he really didn't want the responsibility. Dan thought the GM would fire him, too, if he didn't accept the promotion.

Interpreting Job Ads

Your job search certainly includes looking at advertised positions on job search websites. Therefore, being able to interpret job ads is imperative. You need to be able to read between the lines to determine what exactly a job entails before you apply. Refer to the following guide, which provides plain English meanings to the buzzwords and phrases that are common in most job ads.

When a job ad says this:	It actually means this:
Fast-paced environment	Extreme chaos and total confusion. People have no idea what they are doing.
Team player	Someone who does whatever he or she is told and never complains.
Dedicated	Be prepared to work long hours and weekends for no additional pay.
Passionate	Being a workaholic with no social life, no family, no friends, and no interests outside of work.
Able to meet tight deadlines	Be prepared to work long hours because sales and management underestimate every project and always make unrealistic promises to customers.

When a job ad says this:	It actually means this:
Multi-task	Cope with nonstop interruptions and never be allowed to finish anything.
Results oriented	Expect to finish projects on your own without any help from your boss, so you can be blamed when projects fail.
Self-starter/minimal supervision	Someone who gets no direction because the manager is a total scatterbrain.
Competitive salary	The company pays the same dismal salary as third world competitors and will not pay a cent more than they have to.
Customer focused	Be on call 24-7 and must be willing to drop everything at a moment's notice to react to a crisis.
Service oriented	Same as customer focused.
Strong organizational skills	Clean up messes handed down from others. Must be able to make sense out of incomplete and inaccurate information left over from the person in this position who was recently fired.

When a job ad says this:	It actually means this:
Dynamic	Being able to survive in a totally unstable environment where everything is in constant turmoil.
Versatile	Be ready to get dumped on with many unrelated crappy jobs that co-workers don't want to do.
Forward thinking	Being able to look past the fact that the company's products are junk, and their service is terrible.
Thinking outside the box	Things are so bad that the company is near financial ruin unless they find some solutions fast.
Market leader/industry leader	The company has a least one customer and been in business for at least a month.

In addition to being overloaded with the buzzwords listed above, job ads always depict the hiring company to be a first-class organization that strives for excellence (even if the business is a sweatshop or a company in complete turmoil that is losing money). Only the most qualified candidates are supposed to feel worthy of attempting to join such a high-caliber group.

In developing a job ad for a definite position, the HR personnel and hiring department manager create a wish list of qualifications so specific that only a handful of people on the planet meet the criteria (most of the company's existing employees would fail to make the cut). The list contains a hodgepodge of responsibilities that look overwhelming to most job seekers in the field. The intention is to scare off all but the most serious and confident of applicants.

Even though job ads are written to attract only the most capable candidates, you need not be intimidated. Job ads are commonly inflated. Do you remember how you spiced up your resume to make your mundane experience look impressive? Job ads use the same technique. The responsibilities are enhanced to appear more interesting and more important than they really are. If you happen to be hired, you will surely find that 80% of your time is spent on one or two of the responsibilities listed and the other duties are inconsequential. In addition, responsibilities that look interesting will undoubtedly turn out to be low-level grunt work. You may find that a responsibility expressed in the job ad as "Distribute key components to management for development of strategic plans" turns out to be nothing more than serving coffee and doughnuts to managers in meetings.

4. Interviews

The Ultimate Sales Job

The job interview is without question the most critical part of the job-hunting process. Your resume, cover letter, and networking are merely vehicles utilized to get you to the door. A job interview is your chance to convince the gatekeepers at the door to let you in. From here on, you will have to rely on your dazzling personality, charm, and intellect.

Although that may sound frightening, the good news is that you are now competing against only a few people instead of against hundreds that were in the initial selection process. You initiated contact, and the company has responded favorably by requesting your attendance at an interview. They have obviously looked at your resume or heard about you from one of your networking contacts, and the company is interested in learning more about you. The interview is also the time for you to learn more about the job and the company. Based on the interview, the gatekeepers will decide whether to allow you in, and you will decide whether you truly want in.

The job interview is fundamentally a sales opportunity where you try to sell your services to a potential customer—the company that asked you to come in for the interview. These buyers are extremely cautious and frugal, however. They know that the job market is a buyers' market for most occupations.

Sometimes the interview is an exploratory one. No specific job opening exists, but the company was impressed enough with your unsolicited resume that they want to talk to you in person to see if a possible position exists for you within their organization. In situations like this, you have a bit more power because the company is open minded in hearing what you have to offer.

Interviewers ask serious questions in an attempt to evaluate whether you are the right person for the job. They basically want answers to the following questions:

- Do you have the required technical skills to do the job? (They already have a good idea from your resume, but they want to hear it from you in person, and they want more details.)

- Do you have a personality suited to the role? (Even though personality is a poor indicator of future job performance because solemn, introverted people can be just as productive as cheerful, outgoing people.)
- Are you both on the same page as to salary expectations? (In other words, how desperate are you financially?)
- If you are hired, are you going to make them regret it? (Are you going to be a pain in the butt, making a lot of dumb mistakes and annoying everyone around you? Or can they leave you alone and forget about you?)

The seller (you) must try to convince them:
- You have exceptional technical skills, and what you don't already know will be learned quickly because you are incredibly eager.
- You have the most wonderful personality and get along with everyone.
- Your salary is negotiable. You are more interested in accomplishments than in monetary rewards. Still, you are extraordinarily good at your craft and deserve to command a salary in the higher end of the range.
- If you are hired, the company will not regret it.

In essence, you merely need to tell the interviewers what they want to hear (like politicians telling voters what they want to hear to get elected). However, telling interviewers what they want to hear is more difficult than you might imagine because of many unknowns, as illustrated in the next section.

Interview Scenarios

In the job interview stage, you face a few possible scenarios. The most common ones are:

Small Company Interview
Small companies seldom have HR departments, so job interviews are normally conducted by one person—the company owner or a manager who has the power to hire. The questions are generally direct and about the technical nature of the job. (Here is the job. Can you do it?) Small companies have definite advantages and disadvantages.

Small companies offer less bureaucracy, a wider range of responsibilities, and a greater sense of appreciation. However, you are not able to hide from your boss, so getting along with each other is crucial.

Large companies are bureaucratic, impersonal, and non-appreciative, but they typically pay more and offer better benefits. The social aspect is better in large companies, and you can more easily avoid people whom you dislike.

Large Company, Human Resources Interview
Large companies always have HR departments, so the first job interview is often with a sole HR person. This interview is brutal with every question being in the psychological/behavioral category, as the HR interviewer tries to evaluate your personality. You learn very little about the actual job. If you perform well in this interview, you will be asked to come in for a second interview with the actual department manager.

Large Company, Second Interview

The second interview is with the department manager because you already passed the screening by HR. Questions by the department manager usually relate to your experience and skills. You finally learn some details about the actual job. If an HR person sits in on this interview, he or she will ask very few questions.

Headhunter/Recruiter Interview

More and more companies use third party agencies to find employees for them. This is bad news for job hunters because it means extra interviews and the potential for many wasted hours and trips. (I've had as many as four interviews, and I still didn't get the job.) You can't prepare well for an interview with a recruiter because you don't know who their client company is. Therefore, you don't know what the company does or where it is located. However, this interview generally goes well because recruiters are normally pleasant and want to place you to earn their commissions.

Large Company, HR & Department Manager Interview

This interview is highly unpredictable. It sometimes resembles the good cop/bad cop situation in a police interrogation, with one interviewer being a raving maniac and the other one being calm and professional. Sometimes both the HR person and the department manager seem psychotic, and sometimes both interviewers are personable. You are confronted with both types of questions—the psychological/behavioral ones and the technical, work-related ones.

Large Company with Regional Branches Interview

This kind of organization is highly complex with a head office and a number of regional branches. The interviewer is usually a local manager who reports to head office. Elements of a small company are mixed with elements of a large company. You experience the best of both worlds or the worst of both. The person interviewing you could be twenty years old with no authority to do anything other than follow the procedures set up by head office.

Large Company, Group Interview

This interview is awful. Most of the participants are totally bored and uninterested, sitting in silence while one or two ask all the questions. The main parties are totally unprepared. They quickly scan through your resume (sometimes reading it for the first time), and they ask a few silly questions without even looking up. Awkward silences are followed by people asking questions at the same time. After the interview, you immediately head to the nearest bar. Sometimes the interview is so bizarre, you leave scratching your head in disbelief.

I once had a group interview with four engineers who ran their department as a committee. I was working for another company at the time, so I showed the interviewers some samples of work I had done in the design of a prototype product. They all stared in amazement and couldn't believe that I had time to work on prototypes in my job. Everything they designed was rushed into production without prototyping or testing. I got the impression that all four of them hated their jobs, and they all would apply for my job the minute I left. Needless to say, I stayed where I was.

Why Are They Hiring?

Job openings are the result of one of three situations:
1. Someone quit, retired, or was fired, and that person needs to be replaced.
2. The company is busy (increased business activity or new projects), and the existing staff can't handle the workload.
3. The company has a problem (with systems, processes, equipment, logistics, quality, marketing, finance, personnel, etc.) that needs solving, and their existing employees lack the time or the expertise to solve the problem.

In the interview, you need to find out why the position is available. This knowledge is extremely important to you because fundamentals of the job depend on the reason for hiring.

If the interview is for a specific job opening resulting from an employee leaving, the interviewers have a definite idea of the type of person they want or don't want. If the departed employee was highly competent, they want to replace that person with someone similar. If you have a significantly different personality and skill set than the employee who left, especially if the person was a stellar performer, you are at a distinct disadvantage. You are thoroughly compared to their former star employee in all respects. (Although you seem pretty good, you are not Jennifer.)

On the other hand, if the person leaving was incompetent, the company wants someone much different. In that case, you have an advantage. If you can demonstrate that you are sufficiently competent, you have a good chance of succeeding. (You seem pretty good—much better than that idiot Jason.)

For those reasons, you need to ask why the person left the position and how long that person was doing the job, especially when you contemplate leaving a job. Interviewers are usually quite uncomfortable revealing this information. When asked, they normally say the person left to pursue another opportunity. Why? Was it a compensation issue? Workload? Personality conflicts? Observe the body language of the interviewers when they respond, just as they observe your body language during your answers to their questions. You want to have a clear idea of what you might be stepping into because you don't want to accept a worse job than you already have.

When you are replacing someone, the job duties are more structured, which may or may not be to your liking. The company is more apt to move promptly on hiring, as well. Should you be hired, you will likely be immersed in work from the start and expected to be up to speed quickly. If you prefer to ease into things slowly, you may find this position somewhat stressful.

If the interview is for a new position created because of increased business activity or a new project (the department is super busy and they need help), the interviewers may be more open to seeing what a good candidate can offer. Although you might be compared to others who are doing a similar job in the company, you won't have to fill the shoes of someone who just left. These positions are usually the best for several reasons:
- You do not inherit someone else's entire job (although you may get dumped on with some crappy jobs that co-workers try to unload).
- You generally have more time to ease in and learn the ropes.

- You may be better able to influence the direction your career takes.
- Expanding companies are highly profitable, and they regularly spend like drunken sailors. The growing pains can cause chaos, but to quote the words of one of my former co-workers, "Chaos is cash!"
- If you are a slacker, more opportunities exist for goofing off (not that I would encourage such behavior).

The downside is that the company may take a long time in making a hiring decision because they do not feel the same sense of urgency as they do when replacing someone.

In the last situation, the company has a problem that needs fixing. This presents a great opportunity for you. However, it could also turn out to be a disaster. Points to consider are:

- You are not directly compared to anyone because you are not replacing anybody. No one else is doing the job right now.
- If you succeed, you could be a hero or heroine and enjoy all the associated rewards (or have no reward as others take credit for your success). If you fail, though, you could be out on the street leaving behind a financially wounded company that forever despises you (which isn't so bad, as I have discovered).
- Why does the company have this problem to begin with? Mismanagement is frequently the cause. You could be inheriting a mess and dealing with a lot of future frustration trying to work within the mayhem of a thoroughly dysfunctional organization.
- The company may not be profitable but is hiring anyway in an attempt to make a turnaround. Unprofitable companies are

highly unstable. I know. Most of the companies I worked for lost money and are no longer in business (not because of me, of course, although I like to think I contributed).

Interview Steps

A typical job interview lasts thirty to sixty minutes and moves through the following steps:

1. You arrive early, dressed suitably for the type of position, and announce your arrival to the receptionist or person who first greets you.
2. They make you wait ten minutes. During this time, you should make a preliminary appraisal of the company. After all, you are interviewing them, too. Most people forget that, particularly interviewers, who are often arrogant in assuming that every applicant is a lowly beggar desperate for a job. (Even though that may be true, they don't have to gloat about it!)
3. Finally, one of the interviewers greets and escorts you to a conference room or an office. This person initiates some small talk, banter about the weather and such, to make you feel more at ease. You may be introduced to others attending the interview. Then the torture begins.
4. The main interviewer starts by explaining a bit about the company (information you should already know if you researched the company's website before the interview).
5. The questioning begins with the psychological/behavioral questions:
   - Tell me about yourself. (I'm looking for a job.)
   - What made you apply here? (You advertised for a job.)
   - What are you looking for? (A job.)

6. Of course, you cannot answer step #5 with such direct, truthful answers as shown in parentheses. You must respond with more flowery, convoluted statements. You will learn about proper responses later.
7. After you have answered the first few questions, the interviewers have often made up their minds. The rest of the interview is basically filler to confirm their initial assessment.
8. They ask numerous questions about your education, experience, and achievements. You are asked how you would react to a hypothetical situation. ("How do you handle stress?" Don't answer, "By drinking heavily.") At this point, you still don't know any of the details about the job except what was written in the job posting.
9. After the interviewers have completely exhausted you with questions (many of which are irrelevant), they begin to tell you details about the job they are trying to fill. In many instances, the actual job is significantly different from how it was represented in the job advertisement. At this point, your brain says, "I don't want to do that!" Your body language gives you away as you nod quietly with a glum face and eyes drooping in obvious disappointment while they continue to explain the details of the job. Your enthusiasm has vanished along with any hope of getting this job.
10. After the interview ends, the interviewers thank you and escort you out. You will likely never hear from them again.

In one incident, I had a job interview where I was able to observe the entire office while waiting. About ten people were working in the office, and no one spoke, smiled, or acknowledged my presence. Each and every one of them looked miserable. In addition, I plainly heard the constant boom, boom, boom from machinery in the factory.

I made up my mind before the interview started that I didn't want the job, but I went through the motions anyway. When I was asked what my salary expectations were, I gave some huge figure that made the manager's eyes open wide and his mouth drop. I never heard from them again.

I previously had a manager who made up his mind about hiring a person before the interview even began. If he saw an applicant drive up in a dirty, old, or dented car, the person had no chance of getting a job in our department. My manager believed that driving a dirty or rundown car was indicative of laziness and showed a lack of pride.

In an interview, a company asks many questions about your experience and wants to hear examples of your innovation and creativity. That is the only time a company wants to hear about your previous jobs. Once hired, your new employer does not want to hear a word about how you did things at your old job. They usually just want you to shut up and follow procedures.

A Winning Strategy

In a typical interview, interviewers coerce a job hunter into talking first. If you are an inexperienced, unsuspecting job hunter, you can easily shoot your mouth off before you even know what the job is or what the interviewers are looking for. This technique is intentional on the part of the interviewers. Like a poker game, they want you to show your hand before they show theirs. To gain an advantage, you must try to learn a bit about the job details before you say too much and disqualify yourself. Getting the interviewers to talk first is sometimes impossible, but other times it's remarkably easy.

> *In one occurrence, I had an interview with an HR person and a manager who talked continuously. I hardly said anything. The manager babbled for 45 minutes while the HR person sat quietly. I listened intently and smiled occasionally. I got the job despite speaking for only about a minute. I guess the manager liked the fact that I was a good listener and didn't interrupt his incessant blathering.*

If you can maneuver them into talking first, you can learn a few details about the actual job. Then you can provide answers that they want to hear. For example, if I learn the job involves working with a small group of people, I say that I **love** working in small teams because I can do a wide variety of tasks. If I discover that I will be working with a large group of people, I say that I **love** working in large teams because I can focus my energy and abilities on specialized tasks. The truth is I have no preference; I can do either. To me, both are equally unpleasant.

If the job hours are 7:00 a.m. to 3:30 p.m., I tell the interviewer, "Great, I like to get up early." If the job hours are 9:00 a.m. to 5:30 p.m., I tell the interviewer "Great, I prefer to work late." The truth is I hate getting up early, but I also hate working late. My preference is actually 10:00 a.m. to 2:00 p.m., but companies never offer that alternative.

Not only do you have to tell interviewers what they want to hear, you also have to display body language that they want to see. To succeed in an interview, you sometimes must fake enthusiasm for work that is distasteful and/or unchallenging, as well as pretend to be excited about work that is too challenging and overwhelming.

On rare occasions, however, you may be confronted with a job opportunity that you are genuinely thrilled about—a chance to do something that you might truly enjoy doing. Such opportunities are gems that you need to capitalize on because they are rare in a world full of mediocre jobs.

Unless you have an unblemished job history, being completely frank and direct in an interview more often than not results in failure to receive a job offer. I don't like the fact that the job interview process has evolved into a psychological head game, but it has. You must remember several points:

- Job interviews are sales opportunities, and propaganda and exaggeration are key attributes in selling. If you are trying to sell a new luxury car and tell the truth to prospective customers (the new car is overpriced, unreliable, and impractical), you will never make a sale. Instead, you tell prospective customers that the new luxury car is advanced, sophisticated, and affordable.
- Job interviews are partly poker games, and bluffing is an expected tactic in a poker game.
- Your competitors, without question, are making every effort to get the job. If you are the only honest one in a group of shrewd and cunning candidates, you lose.

- The interviewers are also using sales techniques to promote their company as a great place to work. They emphasize that excellence and high standards are pervasive throughout their organization, and they claim that their employees are highly competent and cooperative. Hardly. I've heard stories of such mythical organizations, but I've never witnessed it firsthand. You won't know for sure what a company is like until you are hired, but you can be certain it will not be anywhere near as efficient as the interviewers portray it to be.

A manager told me in an interview that the cost estimates in his department were so accurate that the amount of water used in a shop floor operation was calculated to within a few ounces. After I was hired, I related the story to my co-workers. They laughed. In reality, cost estimates were a series of arbitrary guesses combined with a lot of fudged numbers.

Even within the interview game, a definite line exists between being shrewd and being a blatant liar. As well, the distinction between self-promotion and being an egotistical blowhard is quite clear. I do not advocate making outrageous false claims and bragging shamelessly unless you are trying to win the job of president of the USA.

In ordinary job interview situations, you must be subtle. You need to sound positive without sounding fake. You must appear eager and keen without seeming weird. You must be confident but not arrogant or brash. This may take some practice and rehearsal. In the next section, you are presented with some common job interview questions and possible responses.

Interview Questions

In the following quiz, you will be given ten questions that interviewers frequently ask. Select the response that you think is most appropriate.

What kind of job are you looking for?
a. An easy job that pays a lot of money.
b. I am great at everything. What do you have?
c. I am looking for a job that allows me to grow personally and professionally as I seek more responsibility and greater challenges while progressing in my career. I want to put my extensive skills and experience to use and help this firm prosper.

Why do you want to work here?
a. I need the money, and I heard this place doesn't suck as much as most companies in this stinking town.
b. I want to play on a last place team—a team of losers like you have working here—and turn it into a winner.
c. This company has an excellent reputation in the industry for quality products and outstanding service. I would be honored and proud to work here.

What can you do for this company?
a. I can be quiet and not get in anybody's way.
b. I can do a much better job than the imbeciles who work here now.
c. I can manage an entire project. I can design the product, build the product, sell the product, and deliver the product to the customer. I can do the purchasing, the accounting, and

the administration. I can dig the raw ore out of the ground with my bare hands and then produce the molten metal with the fires of my spirit and the sweat of my brow. In short, I can do whatever it takes to get the job done on time and within budget.

What are your strengths?
a. I am pretty good at video games.
b. I can lift 200 lbs. over my head without even breathing hard.
c. Perseverance, diligence, dedication, patience, loyalty, creativity, innovation, enthusiasm, and integrity. I am organized, analytical, calm, cheerful, energetic, self-motivated, quick to learn, slow to anger, and fun to be with.

What are your weaknesses?
a. I've been told that I have an odor problem, although I can't really detect it.
b. I sometimes lose my temper, and I will smash and throw things and kick, claw, and spit at people while screaming and hollering obscenities at the top of my lungs.
c. The only real weakness I have is that I tend to work too hard and sometimes lose track of time because I am so involved in my work. However, I am trying to limit myself to twelve-hour workdays. It is difficult, though, because I love working so much. I find that I am bored if I'm not at work.

Where do you see yourself in five years?
a. Thousands of miles away from this God forsaken hellhole of a town.
b. Either having your job or being your boss.
c. I believe I will be an integral part of this company in five

years, possibly in a supervisory position. I see myself as having grown and progressed greatly during those years. I feel that by taking on additional responsibilities and accepting new challenges each and every day, I will have accomplished an enormous amount in that time.

I see that you have had ten different jobs in the past five years. Why did you leave those other jobs?
a. All those companies went broke, and I was laid off.
b. Because all those jobs sucked, and my bosses were idiots.
c. I became uninspired and unchallenged after a short time, and I wasn't learning anything. Better offers kept coming along, so I jumped at the opportunity to work up to my potential.

Why should we hire you over the other candidates?
a. You should hire somebody else because I really don't want to work here. I only came here to satisfy my Unemployment Insurance officer.
b. I am the best thing to have ever walked through your door. If you pass on me, you will be sorry because I will be snapped up by your competition in no time.
c. I believe my unique combination of education, skills, and experience is ideally suited to helping an organization such as this. I can offer tremendous value because I have exceptional credentials and a strong work ethic. Financial compensation is not important to me; my reward is in producing top quality work.

What motivates you?
a. Money. It's the only reason why I work.
b. Winning and power. I love crushing people in competitions,

and I love the feeling I get when people fear me.
c. I am motivated by success in my career and in providing for my family. I receive immense satisfaction from achieving goals within a team environment. Winning as a team is much more rewarding to me than personal accomplishments.

Do you have any references we can call?
a. Unfortunately, no. They all died in the floods.
b. Sure. You might have trouble contacting them, though, because they have limited access to phones in prison.
c. Absolutely. Here are several references that you can call to verify the high caliber of work that I do. I encourage you to call them.

If you selected "c" for each question, you are on the right path to telling interviewers what they want to hear. Keep in mind that some of the "c" examples are exaggerated for comedic effect. You should not portray yourself to be a workaholic or somebody who does not desire adequate financial compensation. Consider that interviewers, like everyone else, are drawn to people who are similar to themselves. Most managers are not workaholics, and they definitely do not work cheap. However, they are ambitious, driven, and career oriented. Therefore, you must present an image of yourself as someone who is focused, energetic, and career minded, even if you are not.

Strange Interviews

Although most interviewers follow the HR interview playbook, sometimes interviewers are so strange you cannot anticipate their questions or their peculiar behavior. I have already shared a few true stories with you in the previous sections, but two other bizarre interviews I experienced are particularly memorable.

I had an interview one time with an engineering manager in a medium-sized manufacturing company who gave me a questionnaire to take home, fill out, and bring back the next day. I don't recollect all the questions, but some were math questions, some were questions asking how I would tackle certain technical problems, and some were spelling questions. Spelling? How odd! I could simply look up the words on a computer or dictionary to find the correct spelling.

I returned the following day and spoke with the manager. He quickly looked over my questionnaire, and then he offered me a job as a technical writer. I had never done technical writing before, and I was completely unfamiliar with the company's products. The truly strange part, though, was that he wanted me to work alone after hours when everyone else had gone home. He was too creepy, so I declined.

Another time, I dropped off a resume in person with a medium-sized manufacturing company, and I was able to speak briefly with the production manager. It was Tuesday. He asked me to come back for an interview on Thursday at 4:00 p.m.

I returned on Thursday, but as I was driving into the parking lot, I saw him climb into a car with two other people. I watched as they drove off. I was a bit puzzled and naturally assumed I had come at the wrong time. I walked into the office anyway and spoke with the receptionist. She looked up the manager's calendar and found that he had indeed scheduled my interview for 4:00 p.m. that day. She was unsure where he had gone or when he would return, so I waited.

At 4:30 p.m., the receptionist left for the day and advised that I should leave as well. She didn't come right out and say that the manager was a jerk, but she certainly inferred that he was an awful person, and she implied that I would be wise to avoid working for him.

The manager finally returned at 4:45 p.m., and he made no apology for keeping me waiting for 45 minutes. He was exceptionally rude and arrogant. I was not impressed. I talked to him briefly as he gave me a quick tour through the plant. I left and immediately stroked this company off my list while thinking to myself, "Wow, if this guy behaves like this with job candidates, how bad does he treat the people who actually work for him?"

Other Ramblings

If an interview is going particularly bad, do not feel obligated to stay until the end. Like watching a bad movie, you have no obligation to see how it ends. You already know how a bad interview ends—you are not getting the job. You may not even want the job, so why waste more time than is necessary? Just be direct, explain that you are not right for the job and vice versa, and end the interview. Thank the people involved and leave. I have done it before, and it feels empowering. The interviewers may be stunned, but they will probably appreciate your honesty.

Not every interview goes badly, however. Sometimes you feel that you nailed it, and you are ecstatic. Your performance was worthy of an acting award, and a juicy job offer awaits. Surprisingly, you may not receive the anticipated call despite having a good interview. Other times, you may get a job offer after having a seemingly second-rate interview. It depends entirely on how well or how poorly your competitors did.

Statistically, you need to suffer through five interviews before getting a decent job offer. As well, according to estimates, you must send out 10-20 resumes before being granted an interview. This means that you may need to send out 50-100 resumes to receive a suitable job offer.

With many occupations, though, sending out 50-100 resumes is quite unrealistic. In many communities, you may have only several companies that are potential employers for those in your field. For example, if you are a dental hygienist living in a community with only four dental offices, what do you do if none of them are hiring? Months may pass before a position becomes available, and your skills may erode if not used regularly (as well as your finances eroding). You probably have to move to another city.

The modern workforce is, therefore, highly mobile and becoming increasingly urban. A larger city may have forty dental offices, so the chances of a dental hygienist finding employment are greatly increased. However, ten times as many dental hygienists will be looking for work. It is still a game of musical chairs, except more chairs and more participants are in the game in larger cities.

Your contacts can truly provide an edge in the musical-chairs/job-hunting game. By networking, you might be able to obtain an interview by sending out several resumes instead of 100 resumes. Your contacts can inform you when chairs become open. Before long, you might be able to give up your old, shabby, worn-out chair and sit in one that is in much better condition.

Some experts recommend sending a thank you message to the interviewers after an interview. That's good advice if you truly want the job. It shows the company that you are serious, and it may give you a slight edge over the candidates who did not send a thank-you note.

One last point to make about interviews concerns the problem of attending job interviews when you are already employed. You can easily search for a job and send out resumes on your own time. But attending an interview requires taking time off work if you are in a typical Monday-Friday day job. When the situation arises, you will probably tell your boss that you have an appointment (you can be non-specific). You must be cautious to ensure that your manager does not discover that you are attending a job interview.

On more than one occasion, I have seen a co-worker who regularly dressed like a slob come to work one day dressed up. The person would suspiciously leave for an "appointment" in the middle of the day wearing a tie or a suit. Everyone at work suspected this person had a job interview, including the manager.

You will gain nothing by allowing your boss to discover that you are looking for another job. You may think that your boss will empathize with your plight and try to make you happier (offer more money, a better environment, or more interesting tasks). On the contrary, bosses frequently take such matters personally and feel betrayed.

You see, many organizations are structured in a military mold. Managers (like military officers) make the decisions and employees (like soldiers) follow orders. Consequently, having loyal employees (soldiers) is extremely important. It appears hypocritical in the modern business world because corporations display little loyalty themselves to employees, customers, suppliers, or communities. Nevertheless, front-line employees are expected to be loyal, and once your loyalty comes into question, many managers will treat you differently.

One time I made the mistake of telling my boss that I had a job interview, only because I was contemplating a career change. I needed to take time off from work for an interview, and I didn't want to lie saying I had a doctor's appointment. I thought I had a good rapport with my boss, but once he knew about my interview, he made my life difficult and tried to force me out. Within a few weeks, I was training my replacement.

Managers naturally believe they are good leaders, and they want to be admired and respected by their subordinates and peers. Therefore, if a competent employee—a good foot soldier—wants to leave the team, it reflects badly on the leader.

The exception to the rule is when an employee is useless or highly disliked by a manager. In that case, the manager is happy to learn that person is contemplating leaving the team. In fact, the manager may provide encouragement. So, if your manager inadvertently discovers you are looking for another job and says, "Take as much time off as you need for interviews," or "I heard of this great job opportunity that would be perfect for you," or "You don't want to stay here," then maybe you should take the hint and find a new job.

5. You Found a New Job

You received a decent job offer, and you accepted. Well done! If you are unemployed, that means thumbing your nose at all the people who were hounding you to find a job. Skip ahead a few sections and go have a drink. You deserve it! But for those of you who are now working, stick around because you still have some unfinished business to attend to. You have to quit your present job.

Quitting Your Present Job

Quitting your job involves giving your employer adequate notice (two weeks in most instances) that you will be vacating your position. Depending on the job, notice can be given either verbally or in writing. I suggest a simple written letter informing your boss that you will be leaving on a particular date and thanking the company for providing you with employment over the past month, year, decade, or whatever. You need not say where you are going or why. You can mention it if you are moving to a prominent company, and you want your boss and co-workers to be jealous. On the other hand, if you accept a lateral move to another so-so company at a lower pay rate because you yearn for a change, you may not want to bring it up (e.g., you are taking a job cleaning toilets because you hate your office job).

After giving notice, the reaction you receive from your boss varies considerably:

1. Your boss is quiet and unemotional, sometimes to the extent of not caring. If your employer doesn't care that you are leaving, then you know you are making the right decision. It is time to go.
2. Your boss is disappointed and saddened but understanding and supportive. This type of manager does not interpret your announcement as a personal attack and recognizes that you are strictly making a business decision.
3. Your boss is deeply disturbed, even shocked, that you are choosing to leave. This type of manager takes your decision personally and is troubled because your departure could disrupt production and make him or her look bad.
4. Your boss is very happy for you, almost too happy for you. Smiling from ear to ear, your boss shakes your hand and wishes you luck. After you walk out of your manager's office and close the door, you hear someone shout, "Whoopee!" You

also hear the sound of a champagne cork popping and glasses tingling.

After you give notice, don't expect your present employer to offer more money to entice you to stay (especially if your boss's reaction is #4 above). Occasionally, though, a company will make a lucrative counteroffer under special circumstances:

1. You are in a position vital to daily operations, and no one else can perform your job or learn to perform your job in a short timeframe.
2. Your parents own the company, and your boss will be fired for allowing you to leave.

Situation #1 rarely happens in large companies because someone else can always fill in. In addition, the issue of loyalty as discussed earlier comes into question. A small company, on the other hand, may try hard to retain your services because you are more valued.

I was able to obtain a 20% pay increase from a previous employer by receiving a firm job offer from another company and threatening to quit. However, I was one of only two people who could do the work required, and the other person was already extremely busy and had serious health issues.

If you accept a pay increase to stay at your current job (with company X), the company that wants to hire you (company Y) will be fairly upset. By rejecting their job offer, you will have jeopardized your chances for future employment at company Y. You must ask yourself why you were contemplating leaving your job at company X in the first place. Was it solely for financial reasons?

If you accept more money to stay, will you still be happy in a few months' time when the joy of having a higher income wears off?

When quitting your job, you may be tempted to lash out at your boss or your co-workers or both, but you should avoid doing so. The temporary satisfaction gained from sounding off undoubtedly will be regretted in the future. Burning your bridges, as they say, is unwise for many reasons:

- Your new job could turn out to be major disappointment, and you may possibly want your old job back. In essence, you might have left a mediocre job for one that is worse.
- Your former co-workers or boss could be hired by your new company, and to your dismay, you might be working together again someday.
- The company you are leaving behind (company X) may go through a complete restructuring, booting out the useless and incompetent ones. Perhaps in a few years, this presently dysfunctional organization will be transformed, and you might want to return.
- The company now hiring you (company Y) might go bankrupt or be sold or merged with another in the future. The desirable position you accept now could change dramatically, and you may possibly be job hunting again before long. If you left company X on good terms, you could perhaps return or at least use your former co-workers and managers as networking contacts or as references.

Your Last Days

Your last weeks of work either drag by slowly or are a frantic race to finish off projects. Either way, your last weeks are not much fun. Once you know you are leaving, it is extremely difficult to get motivated to come into work (it was hard enough before). Nonetheless, you want to depart favorably, so putting in a reasonable effort is imperative. Your boss will appreciate a professional attitude of trying to earn your pay on your last few days (even though it might be the first time your boss sees you display a professional attitude). Your co-workers and the person replacing you will appreciate you not leaving a mess for them to clean up. You may even be remembered fondly (although it will be short lived because every problem that crops up for the next six months will be blamed on you).

A social function is frequently held when someone leaves a job. The goodbye ceremony can include cake, goodbye cards, a luncheon, and drinks after work. The departing person often gives a speech stating how wonderful it was to have worked in the company and how much he or she will miss it. (If the job is so good, why is the person leaving?) Personally, I find such melodrama to be nauseating. Even more nauseating is seeing the person return in less than two weeks after having an elaborate send-off. (Do I get a refund for the money I donated to help fund the celebration?)

Your last day on the job is the most uncomfortable day at work, even more uncomfortable than your first day. Your first day is filled with optimism as you are introduced to new people, whereas your last day is filled with weirdness as you say goodbye to people who, despite seeing them every day, you do not really know. Your last hour is spent walking around shaking hands repeating the same short conversation over and over again (co-workers wish you luck and ask where you are heading; you embellish your new job and try to make them jealous). You realize that you will never see most of these people again. When you walk out the door of the building, you are unlikely to enter it ever again.

I have experienced the last day of work dozens of times in my life, far more than the average person has. In many cases, my last day couldn't arrive fast enough. However, when my last day finally did arrive, I always felt a strange hollow feeling as I made my way out the door (a feeling that lasted for all of three seconds, mind you).

My final day at one company was most memorable because I was the last person out of the building. That felt extra strange. The company was small, and I had worked there about six years. I was trying to finish off some things on a Friday afternoon in an effort to help the remaining staff members, but the people I was trying to help all left early.

By 4:00 p.m., the entire building was vacant, except for me. I had given my key to one of the last people to leave, so I could exit the building but not re-enter. At 4:30 p.m., I shut off the lights and carried a box of personal belongings out to my car, which was sitting alone in an otherwise empty parking lot.

After leaving your old job, you should feel excited, albeit somewhat apprehensive about your new job. You may feel the urge to go on a shopping spree. You probably want to buy some new clothes, and you perhaps want to purchase those household items that you have postponed buying for so long. You may even be tempted to look at new cars and different houses. I advise deferring any major purchases until after you have completed a few months at your new job. Your elation in finding fulfilling work may be a bit premature because your new job could turn out to be vastly different from what you had envisioned.

The First Day in Your New Job

The first day on a new job is always an anxious time. The day primarily involves getting oriented with your new surroundings and being introduced to the people who you are going to work with.

If you are replacing someone, your new employer should be ready for you. If you are an office worker, this means having an assigned workspace with a desk and a computer with applicable software installed. You may even take over the vacating person's desk complete with dust bunnies, coffee stains, and stacks of work.

If you are in a new position, having a functioning workspace already set up is a good sign. Unfortunately, your employer may not be ready for you even though they had weeks to prepare and wanted you to start work urgently. Many companies are highly disorganized. On your first day, you may not have a desk, or you might not have a computer. Alternatively, you may have a desk and computer, but you do not have the applicable software installed. Another possibility is that you are unable to use the installed software because of a lack of software licenses (common with newly hired engineering people). Perhaps you are off to a bad start, but don't fret. This is only your first day. At least your new company was expecting you.

In the past, I worked for a pompous, domineering manager, Peter. Peter was always hiring and firing people on a whim. On one occasion, he hired a young technologist without informing anyone else that he had done so. The new technologist showed up for work on a Monday morning, and no one was expecting him. Worse yet, Peter was out of town the whole week. We had no idea why the new person was hired because we had nothing for him to do. He quit after three days. When Peter returned and learned of the fiasco, he shrugged his shoulders uncaringly.

Soon after your arrival, you find out who your immediate supervisor is. Surprisingly, this person may not have attended any of the job interviews you had with the company. In fact, it is common in large companies for a manager to interview and hire workers, then delegate the day-to-day responsibilities of training and supervision to a supervisor or team leader. Therefore, you may seldom speak to or even see the manager who hired you. All your sweet talk about accomplishments in the job interview is meaningless now.

Your immediate supervisor or team leader, who you may be meeting for the first time, is the person who greatly influences whether you are going to enjoy your new job or despise it. He or she is the person who will guide and direct you and be your go-to person for questions. In many circumstances, the immediate supervisor is a highly knowledgeable person who is competent in doing the actual work but not a particularly good teacher.

Although you likely won't do much on your first day, some events can occur that are key indicators of what's to come. As mentioned earlier, a company that is prepared for your arrival is a good sign. On my first day in one job, my new manager had a written checklist of items to go over, and the common questions and concerns of a new employee were addressed. I was impressed.

Unfortunately, most of my first days required me to ask about virtually everything. Where can I park? Where are the bathrooms? Where is the coffee? Where can I get a pen and some paper? How do I get in touch with an IT person because nothing on my computer is working? How do I go about getting a chair that isn't broken because this one is missing a wheel? (When someone quits an office job, the remaining employees typically loot the departing person's workspace taking away the good chair and leaving behind a broken chair for the new hire.)

In a new job as a customer service rep, I had 43 emails on my first day. It was a bad omen because it turned out to be an awful job involving nine-to-ten-hour workdays but being paid for only eight hours.

My most unforgettable first day occurred in the late 1980's. Soon after arriving at work, I was introduced to my supervisor, a feisty immigrant from the former country of Czechoslovakia (this was still in the cold-war days). We spoke briefly, and then he launched into a tirade about the company.

He said, "This is the worst f**king company in the world. It's even worse here than working in communist countries."

Hearing his "motivational" speech on Day 1 surprised me (it usually takes a few days before hearing the complaints). But he was absolutely right. It turned out to be a dreadful place to work.

The First Weeks in Your New Job

After your first few weeks on the job, you should have some indication of what your job is, and you should have some inkling as to the corporate culture. By now, you should have answers to the following questions:

- Is the company rigid with employees watching the clock, or is the culture more flexible with people coming and going in a relaxed manner?
- Do your co-workers work regular-length days, or do they put in a lot of overtime?
- Do you hear a lot of idle chatter and personal conversations or are the discussions mostly work related?
- Do you hear people laugh, or is the environment exceedingly sober?
- Does work appear to flow in an orderly manner, or is the environment extremely turbulent?
- Do co-workers quietly go about their business, or do they complain constantly?
- Is the job what you expected, or is it quite different from what was represented in your interview(s)?
- Are your co-workers long-term employees, or does the company have a high employee turnover rate?

I had recently started a new job and noticed someone was quitting every second week. I commented to a co-worker about it, and he said the turnover rate had really decreased. Someone used to quit every week.

I once worked beside a fellow, Greg, who quit after 2-1/2 days. He walked out in the middle of the day without saying a word to anybody, and he never returned.

The department manager phoned Greg to find out what had happened, and Greg said that he left that day because another employee, Mel, had been staring at him. Mel habitually gazed into space, deep in thought, but Greg thought Mel was staring at him, so he quit.

At a large company many years ago, I sat near a new employee, Doug, who worked for a couple of weeks then failed to show up for work. Nobody knew where he was. Weeks passed by, and there was still no word about Doug. Was he sick? Did he quit? Did he die? No one knew for sure.

After about a month, a manager who sat nearby finally noticed and asked about him. We told the manager (he wasn't Doug's boss) that we hadn't seen him in weeks. The manager was puzzled because he didn't know who hired Doug or what his job was. To this day, I don't know what happened to Doug, but he was probably paid for a month without showing up. He might still be getting paid.

After a month or two in your new job, you should be feeling one of the following:

- Happy. You are starting to feel comfortable with the work, your new co-workers, and your boss. The job so far is interesting and at a suitable pace to your liking.
- Overwhelmed. You have so much to learn and so much work to do. You find it extremely stressful.
- Bored. You have virtually nothing to work on, and your immediate supervisor is too busy and too disorganized to assign you any work. The days drag on as you try to look busy. You even resort to reading the unbearably dull policy and procedure manuals.
- Bewildered. You have no clue what you are supposed to do. You have been given no direction or guidance, and nobody seems to know what you should be working on.
- Depressed. You hate this job already.

If you are feeling happy, great! You may have stumbled onto a higher quality mediocre job or possibly even a good job. You could be experiencing stable employment and enjoying a steady income for years to come.

Instead, if you are feeling overwhelmed, bored, bewildered, or depressed in your new job, you shouldn't do anything drastic yet (like beg for your old job back). You must wait and see if conditions improve as you become more comfortable and familiar with your duties. Sometimes the job becomes more tolerable; other times it gets worse.

The Cycle Repeats

The story doesn't end here just because you have a job and you are at the end of the book. If your new job turns out to be a disappointment, you are apt to be looking for a job again in short order. Even if you are reasonable happy now, the probability is high that you will be looking for a job again sometime in the future. Whether you become dissatisfied with the work, the salary, the company, or the people, you are sure to become uninspired in this job at some point, and you will likely seek a better opportunity.

Another possibility is that an economic downturn or corporate restructuring forces you to look for work in the future. In the past, a company eliminated jobs as a last resort after suffering huge financial losses. But in the modern world, even a profitable corporation will cut jobs if profits are lower than expected. The future is highly unpredictable. Therefore, having good job-hunting skills is of prime importance in this volatile world.

However, being able to find a job is only one part of the equation for career survival. You don't want to be looking for a new job every few months, so you must be able to endure the chaos of the modern workplace for some period in between job searches. For that reason, I am compelled to write another book—one to help people function in this growing environment of corporate dysfunction. If you found this book to be somewhat useful or mildly entertaining, please keep an eye out for my next book. (It's another shameful promotion, I know.)